Isaac Asimov's

21st Century

Library of the Universe

Near and Far

The Life and Death of Stars

BY ISAAC ASIMOV
WITH REVISIONS AND UPDATING BY RICHARD HANTULA

Gareth Stevens Publishing
A WORLD ALMANAC EDUCATION GROUP COMPANY

Please visit our web site at: www.garethstevens.com
For a free color catalog describing Gareth Stevens Publishing's list of high-quality
books and multimedia programs, call 1-800-542-2595 (USA) or 1-800-387-3178 (Canada).
Gareth Stevens Publishing's fax: (414) 332-3567.

Library of Congress Cataloging-in-Publication Data

Asimov, Isaac.
  The life and death of stars / by Isaac Asimov; with revisions and updating by Richard Hantula.
    p. cm. — (Isaac Asimov's 21st century library of the universe. Near and far)
  Includes bibliographical references and index.
  ISBN 0-8368-3967-6 (lib. bdg.)
  1. Stars—Juvenile literature. I. Hantula, Richard. II. Asimov, Isaac. Star cycles. III. Title.
QB801.7.A855   2002
523.8'8—dc22   2004057842

This edition first published in 2005 by
Gareth Stevens Publishing
A WRC Media Company
330 West Olive Street, Suite 100
Milwaukee, WI 53212 USA

Series editor: Mark J. Sachner
Cover design and layout adaptation: Melissa Valuch
Picture research: Mathew Groshek
Additional picture research: Diane Laska-Swanke
Production director: Jessica Morris

The editors at Gareth Stevens Publishing have selected science author Richard Hantula to bring
this classic series of young people's information books up to date. Richard Hantula has written
and edited books and articles on science and technology for more than two decades. He was
the senior U.S. editor for the *Macmillan Encyclopedia of Science*.

In addition to Hantula's contribution to this most recent edition, the editors would like to
acknowledge the participation of two noted science authors, Greg Walz-Chojnacki and
Francis Reddy, as contributors to earlier editions of this work.

Printed in the United States of America

1 2 3 4 5 6 7 8 9 09 08 07 06 05

Contents

We live in an enormously large place – the Universe. It's only natural that we would want to understand this place, so scientists and engineers have developed instruments and spacecraft that have told us far more about the Universe than we could possibly imagine.

We have seen planets up close, and spacecraft have even landed on some. We have learned about quasars and pulsars, supernovas and colliding galaxies, and black holes and dark matter. We have gathered amazing data about how the Universe may have come into being and how it may end. Nothing could be more astonishing.

We have also come to understand that the Universe changes. It may not seem to be changing, because the events can happen so slowly. For instance, stars come into being, change with time, and grow older. All this happens over a great deal of time. Eventually, the stars come to an end, sometimes in violent ways.

A Star Is Born

Stars are born within giant gas clouds. Gas and dust swirl deep in these clouds. This action forms pockets of gas. Deep in one cloud, a pocket of gas grows large enough that its gravity pulls more gas into it. Gradually, its center begins to contract, and it warms up.

The pocket of gas spins slowly at first, but then it spins ever faster. The swirling gas flattens into a disk. Eventually, its hot central part begins to produce energy on its own − and a star is born. It may remain hidden within the cloud for millions of years, but it will emerge. Perhaps planets will form before the young star's energy blows the surrounding disk away.

In another part of the same great dark gas cloud, an older star has reached the end of its ability to produce energy. It suddenly collapses and then explodes, returning its material to the cloud from which it was born. The powerful blast stirs up the gas and creates new pockets − and perhaps new stars.

Above: Out of this cool, dark gas cloud somewhere in the Galaxy, a star has begun to form out of a clump of gas.

The young star grows as its gravity gathers more gas from the surrounding cloud.

A Stellar Nursery

The Orion Nebula is one of the closest regions of recent star formation. It is about 1,500 light-years from Earth. Hot, young stars at its center supply the energy that makes its gas glow.

The Orion Nebula, which is about 30 light-years wide, is only a small part of a cloud that spans an entire constellation. Dust in the cloud blocks the light of the young stars within it, but the dust is warmed by those stars. Instruments sensitive to heat can detect the warmth. The colorful Orion Nebula is really just a bubble of gas blown off of this great invisible gas cloud. The stars that make the Orion Nebula shine have only just broken out of their nursery.

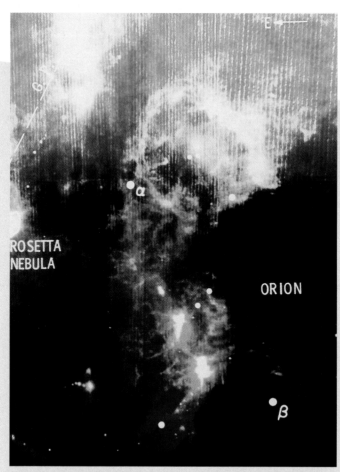

Above: The *Infrared Astronomical Satellite* made this map of the vast Orion Molecular Cloud. The brightest areas are the hottest. The bright area just below the center of the image is the Orion Nebula.

Below: A cluster of hot, young stars in the center of the Orion Nebula causes its gas to glow.

Inside the Orion Nebula

A cluster of four young, very bright stars has formed near the edge of the star-forming region in the Orion Nebula. These stars, called the Trapezium, are hotter and brighter than our Sun. They are so hot that most of the energy they give off is ultraviolet radiation, not visible light.

This ultraviolet radiation has a great effect on the nebula. It causes the gas surrounding the stars to glow green, blue, red, and yellow up to a distance of five light-years away. Great shock waves ripple outward from the Trapezium as gas heated by the stars collides with cooler gas. These waves create the delicate wisps and filaments we see in the nebula.

Many of the young stars are surrounded by dusty disks of material. How many planets might there be in the Orion Nebula?

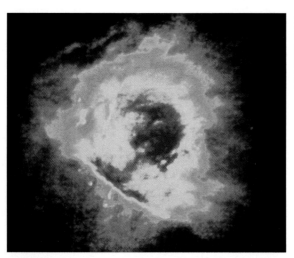

Left: This image from the Very Large Array radio telescope reveals a web of stringlike filaments in the center of the Orion Nebula around the hot Trapezium stars.

Multiple stars — not as odd as you might think!

Often a cloud of gas will collapse not into a single star but into two or more closely spaced stars that orbit each other. When such multiple-star systems were first discovered, they were believed to be rare. Now scientists think that at least half of all stars are multiple. What makes a cloud condense into a single star or into multiple stars, and how does that influence the formation of planets? Scientists do not yet know.

Above: A close-up view of the central region of the Orion Nebula.

Our Average Sun

Stars come in all sizes. Our Sun is larger than the majority of stars. Once a star forms, the heat it produces by nuclear fusion expands it enough to offset its gravitational pull, so it doesn't shrink. The star remains stable and doesn't change very much for millions of years or more, depending on the type of star.

Our Sun has been shining for about four and a half billion years and is only middle-aged. It will keep shining more or less as it is for several billion more years. The hydrogen at its center changes slowly to helium, and the heat produced gives us light and warmth and makes it possible for life to exist on Earth.

Above: Many stars have partners. The Sun, the star on which life on Earth depends, is a single star.

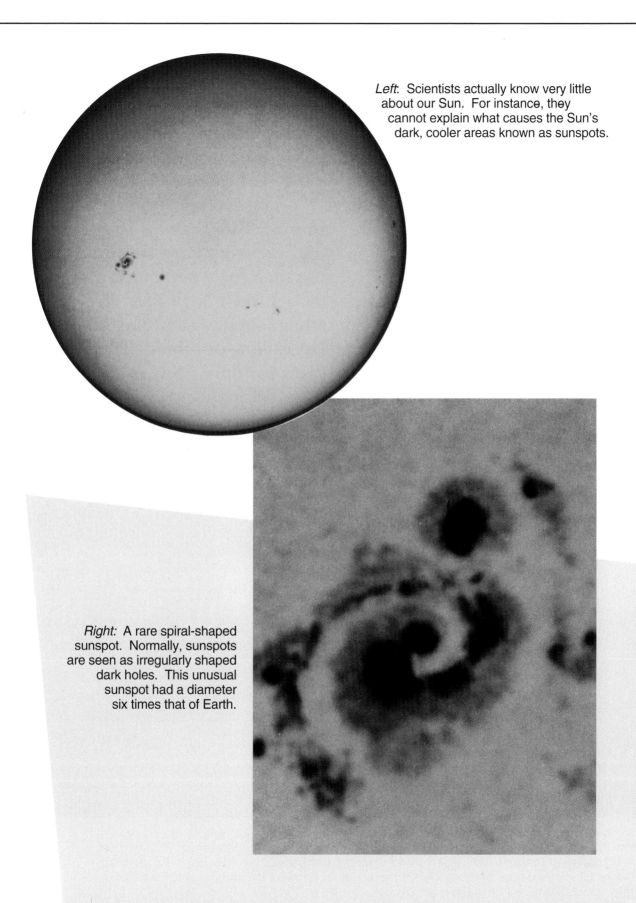

Left: Scientists actually know very little about our Sun. For instance, they cannot explain what causes the Sun's dark, cooler areas known as sunspots.

Right: A rare spiral-shaped sunspot. Normally, sunspots are seen as irregularly shaped dark holes. This unusual sunspot had a diameter six times that of Earth.

The Brilliance of the Stars

Most stars are both smaller and cooler than our Sun and shine with a dim red light. But some stars are larger, hotter, and more luminous than the Sun. The star Rigel in the constellation Orion, for example, is about 50,000 times as luminous as the Sun. Scientists reported in 2004 that a star called LBV 1806-20 has about 150 times the mass of our Sun and may be as much as 40 million times as luminous. This star is located in our Galaxy, about 45,000 light-years from us, but it cannot be seen with the naked eye, because it lies behind a cloud of gas and dust.

In order to remain as bright as they are, very large stars must use their hydrogen quickly. Even though their large sizes give them a huge supply, such stars do not last as long as others. They may shine for only a few million years before using up their hydrogen.

1   2   3   4

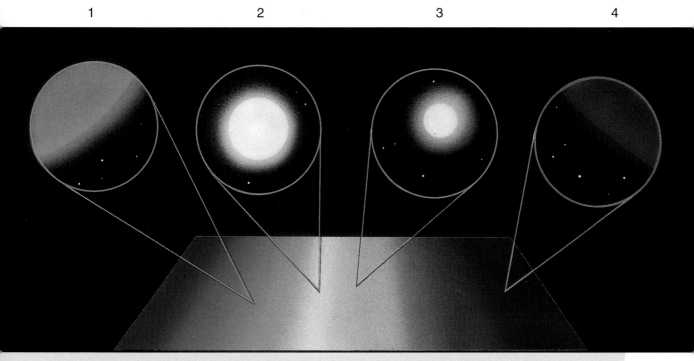

Above: The color of light a star produces depends on its mass, age, and temperature. Hot, young, and massive blue-white stars like Lambda Cephei (1) and Sirius (2) burn their fuel quickly. A massive star near the end of its life, like Betelgeuse (4), glows a cooler red but gives off great heat because of its large surface. Our yellow Sun (3), which is smaller and cooler, burns its fuel much more slowly.

Above and below: Different types of stars have different colors caused by different stellar temperatures. Star trails *(above, identified in the diagram below)* display a range of pale, barely detectable colors. The brightest star in the nighttime sky is Sirius.

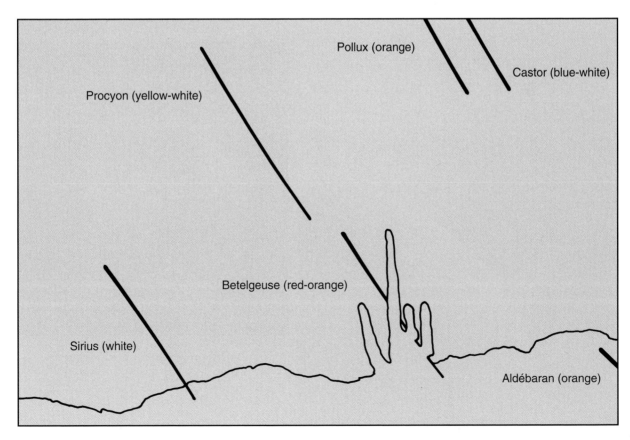

Pollux (orange)

Castor (blue-white)

Procyon (yellow-white)

Betelgeuse (red-orange)

Sirius (white)

Aldébaran (orange)

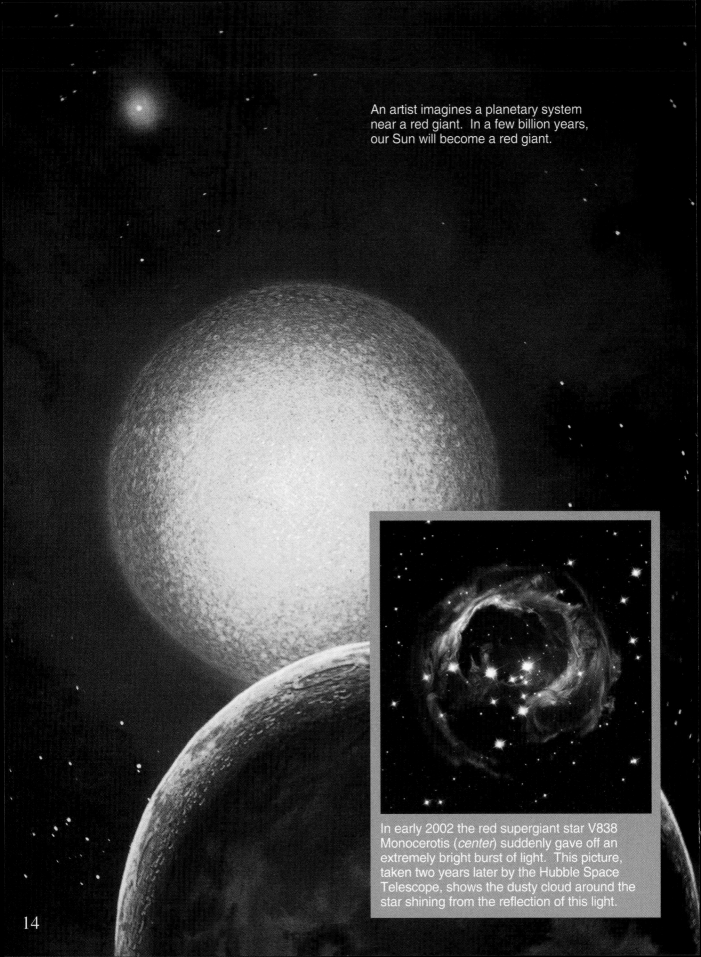

An artist imagines a planetary system near a red giant. In a few billion years, our Sun will become a red giant.

In early 2002 the red supergiant star V838 Monocerotis (*center*) suddenly gave off an extremely bright burst of light. This picture, taken two years later by the Hubble Space Telescope, shows the dusty cloud around the star shining from the reflection of this light.

Giants of the Sky

When a star shines steadily, it is in what is known as the "main sequence." Our Sun is in the main sequence now.

Eventually, a star collects more and more helium in its center. Little is known about what happens to the tiny stars called red dwarfs when they get old. But in the case of other stars, as the hydrogen fuel runs out, the star contracts and squeezes its helium. The central temperature rises until the helium atoms begin to form more complicated atoms – carbon, oxygen, and even heavier elements like iron. The extra heat makes the outer layers of the star expand; the star grows larger and larger. As the outer layers expand, they become cooler and glow red hot. Such stars are called red giants. A star about the size of our Sun becomes a red giant as its hydrogen runs low, but stars somewhat more massive than the Sun become enormous red supergiants.

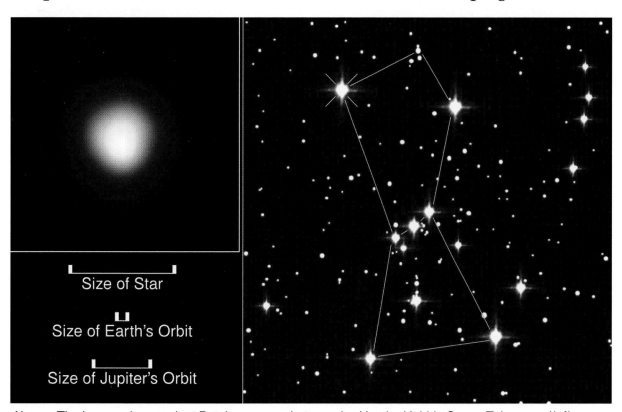

Size of Star

Size of Earth's Orbit

Size of Jupiter's Orbit

Above: The huge red supergiant Betelgeuse as photographed by the Hubble Space Telescope (*left*). Betelgeuse is the upper left star in the diagram of the constellation Orion at *right*.

Supernova — Star Bright

When enough atoms of iron and other heavy elements build up in the center of a very large star, the star can no longer produce energy. Without the fierce heat from its core, it cannot balance its gravity. It collapses suddenly, which creates an explosion that releases tremendous amounts of energy. The star is blown apart!

Scientists believe that only very large stars (and also white dwarfs that attract matter from a nearby companion star) can explode in what is called a supernova. During the explosion, the star's outer layers grow so hot that, for a few weeks, a single supernova will shine as brightly as an entire galaxy of stars.

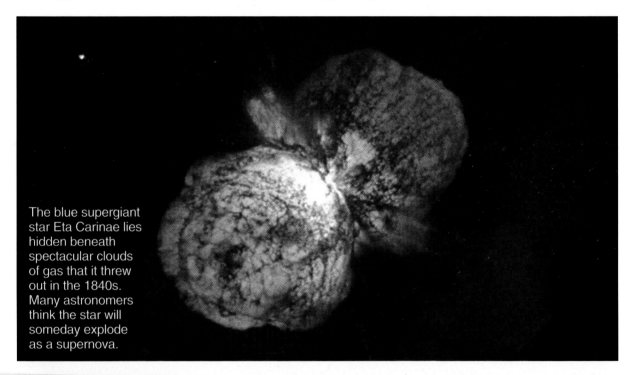

The blue supergiant star Eta Carinae lies hidden beneath spectacular clouds of gas that it threw out in the 1840s. Many astronomers think the star will someday explode as a supernova.

Can supernovas be predicted?

Supernovas always catch us by surprise. If scientists could predict when a star might explode, instruments could be put in place to study the first moments of the explosion and even the time before it. But scientists cannot yet predict supernovas. They know a star has to be in the supergiant stage (or, alternatively, has to be a white dwarf that draws matter from a close companion star), but whether a particular star will explode tomorrow or ten thousand years from now is a puzzle.

Pictured is the Crab Nebula, a remnant of a star that exploded as a supernova in the year 1054. The explosion could be seen in daylight for weeks.

About ten light-years across, the supernova remnant known as Cassiopeia A emits radio waves as it expands into space. This image was made using the Very Large Array radio telescope in New Mexico.

17

The latest known supernova to occur relatively "close" to Earth appeared to astronomers in 1987. The area before the explosion is shown *above*. The photo *below* was taken just after the explosion. The bright new star is not new at all. It is the final burst of light from a large and unstable star.

A Supernova for Our Times

In 1604 a supernova was observed in our Galaxy. For a long time after that, the only supernovas that scientists could detect occurred in far distant galaxies, and they could only be dimly seen through telescopes.

But in 1987 a supernova was seen in the Large Magellanic Cloud, a small galaxy only about 180,000 light-years from our Galaxy's center. It gave out a hundred million times as much power as our Sun. Called Supernova 1987A, it was the closest supernova to Earth in nearly four centuries. For the first time, scientists could use advanced instruments to study a supernova. They studied just how radiation and particles called neutrinos were given off and how a cloud of gas formed and expanded.

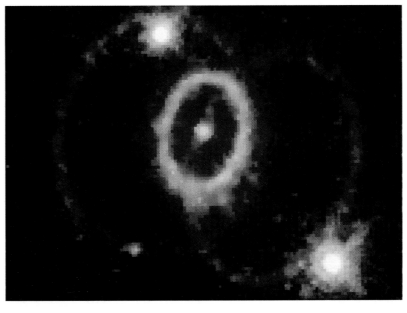

Right: A 1994 picture, made by the Hubble Space Telescope, of the explosion site of Supernova 1987A. Some astronomers think the rings may represent gas thrown out by the star shortly before it became a supernova.

A look back in time

Astronomers saw Supernova 1987A in February 1987, but that is not when the star exploded. The supernova occurred in a small galaxy about 180,000 light-years from us. That means light from it took 180,000 years to reach us. The explosion took place some 180,000 years ago, but the light from it just reached Earth in 1987. Some very distant objects are more than 12 billion light-years away. We see them as they looked more than 12 billion years ago. That's how long it took their light to reach us.

Transforming the Giants

As a star like our Sun collapses, gravity breaks its atoms into smaller pieces and forces them close together. Such a star's material can be squeezed into an object about the size of Earth. This shrunken star is called a white dwarf.

A still larger star collapses more violently, squeezing the pieces of atoms. After a supernova explosion dies down, what was once a giant star can become a tiny, tightly packed ball perhaps only 12 miles (20 km) across. This is a neutron star.

But if the star that exploded was extremely large, its collapse will squeeze the star's material even more tightly together, and the center of the collapsing star will become a black hole.

Below: Weighing a scant 0.00002 pound (0.000009 kg), a cup of average red giant matter (1) would barely lower a scale. A cup of matter from a star like our Sun (2) would weigh 0.73 pound (0.33 kg). The scale would crumble under a 5.1-million-pound (2.3-million-kg) cup of white dwarf matter (3). And a cup of neutron star matter (4) would register an amazing 730 trillion pounds (330 trillion kg) – if you could find a scale to weigh it on!

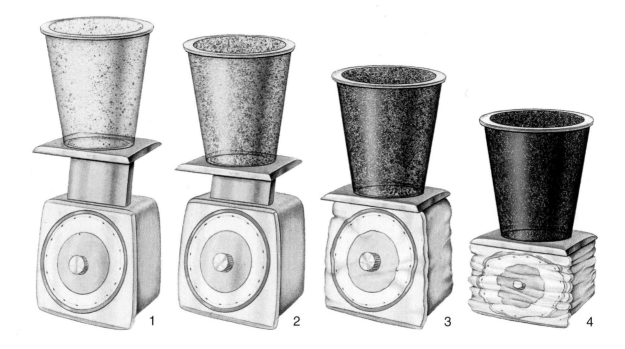

1   2   3   4

The tiny spot at the middle of this picture (made by combining light and X-ray data) is the neutron star at the center of the Crab Nebula. It spins thirty times a second.

Neutron stars — fast and deadly

Neutron stars spin very rapidly, often many times a second. Astronomers have found neutron stars that rotate as fast as six hundred times a second. They have also found neutron stars that circle ordinary stars. With their powerful gravitational pull, the neutron stars slowly draw the material out of the ordinary stars into themselves, destroying the stars.

Life on Earth developed as our Sun settled into its current stage *(above, left)*. In several billion years, when the Sun expands into a red giant, things will change quite a bit. First, the ocean water will turn into vapor, creating thick clouds *(above, right)*. In time, Earth's oceans will boil away. Our planet's crust will soften and begin to melt *(below)*. Before Earth becomes lost in the growing outer layers of the Sun, our neighboring Moon will dissolve *(opposite)*.

Earth's End

Someday our Sun will die, too, or at least it will cease being the kind of star it is now. Several billion years from now, it will start consuming helium in its core. It will start expanding and turning red. The Sun's surface will be cooler than it is now. But as it expands, there will be so much surface that the total amount of heat will become far greater than it is now.

The Sun's increased heat will make life on Earth impossible. Eventually, in fact, the Sun will expand so much that it will swallow Mercury, Venus, and perhaps even Earth. Our planet will no longer exist.

The Final Days of Our Sun

Although Earth will be gone, the Sun will still exist for a time as a red giant. A few hundred million years after it becomes a red giant, the Sun will collapse. It will be too small to collapse violently enough to become a supernova. It will become a white dwarf, scattering its outermost layers in all directions and forming a shell of gas called a planetary nebula. There are some of these already in the sky — white dwarfs shining within a shell of expanding gas.

The Sun will continue to shine as a white dwarf for many billions of years, gradually cooling into what astronomers call a black dwarf, which is a burned-up cinder of a star.

Below and opposite, bottom: **Examples of planetary nebulas. Planetary nebulas are gaseous shells lit up by white dwarfs, the remains of Sun-like stars. They are called planetary nebulas because many of them resemble disks when seen through telescopes.**

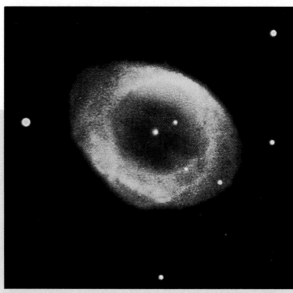

Above: The Ring Nebula in the constellation Lyra.

Below: The Bug Nebula in Scorpius.

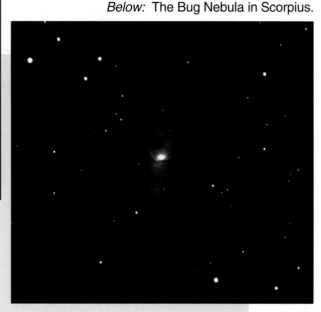

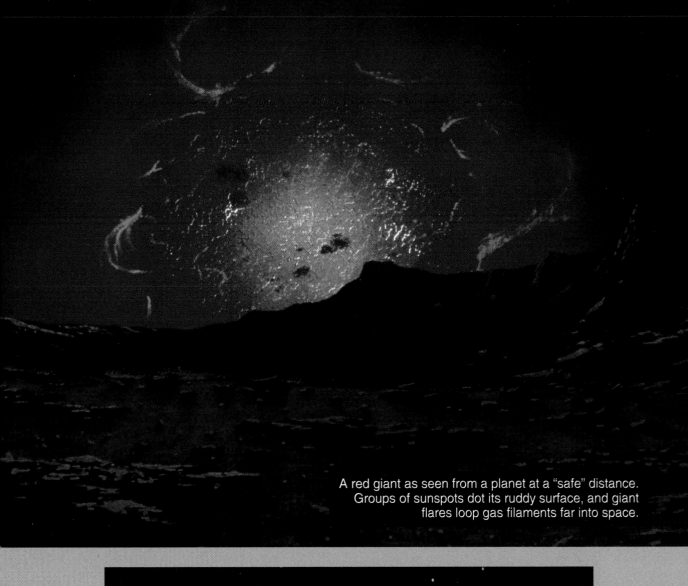

A red giant as seen from a planet at a "safe" distance. Groups of sunspots dot its ruddy surface, and giant flares loop gas filaments far into space.

The Eskimo Nebula in Gemini.

The Hubble Space Telescope sent back this remarkably sharp true-color photo of giant galactic nebula NGC 3603. This view is all the more remarkable for the fact that within it can be found formations indicating stars at various stages of birth, life, and death.

Born of the Stars

Out of the deaths of stars may come the births of other stars. When a supernova explodes, most of its matter is scattered about in space. This matter includes atoms more complicated than those of hydrogen and helium, such as carbon, oxygen, silicon, and iron. The clouds of gas that exist between the stars start to contain these complicated atoms. When new stars form out of these clouds, they too contain some of the complicated atoms.

Because the new stars are "born" out of matter from earlier stars, they are called second-generation stars. Our Sun is an example of a second-generation star. Scientists think that earlier stars could only have planets made up of simple atoms — mainly hydrogen and helium. Only second-generation stars can have planets made of rock and metal, like Earth. And since the complicated atoms that make up much of our bodies also came from ancient stellar matter, we, too, are "born" of the stars!

Above: The next time you take a stroll beneath the Milky Way, imagine the stars as your cosmic birthplace.

Children of the stars

Scientists think that after the Big Bang, only simple atoms — mainly those of hydrogen and helium — formed. Atoms more complex than these formed later in the centers of stars. These complex atoms were then spread throughout space by giant supernova explosions. Our planet Earth and our own bodies are made up largely of these complex atoms. This means that many atoms in our planet and ourselves were formed at the center of some star that once exploded violently. We are children of the stars.

Fact File: Starlight

All stars are born approximately the same way. But their sizes and masses affect how long they live, and also how they die.

The smallest red dwarfs are less than a tenth the size of our Sun, while the largest supergiant stars are millions of times bigger than the Sun. The chart on these two pages shows time estimates suggested by some astronomers for various stages in the lives of three different kinds of stars. These three "typical" stars are the following: a giant star with

Time from Nebula Stage	Giant Star (15 solar masses)	Average Star (1 solar mass)	Small Star (1/3 solar mass)
100,000 years	Matter contracts into large ball. Resulting giant star has a lot of matter but burns very quickly.		
1 million years		Matter contracts into hot core; protostar forms – about 20 times Sun's brightness and width.	
10-20 million years	Helium created by nuclear fusion begins to build up in core. Star feeds on helium and becomes red supergiant; it soon explodes in a supernova. Tiny – maybe only 12 miles (20 km) wide – but massive neutron star remains.	Hydrogen atoms in star begin the fusion process. Protostar becomes a star.	Temperature inside the core of the nebula that will give birth to a red dwarf is just high enough to start burning. Low temperature means future red dwarf star will burn its hydrogen slowly and "live" longer than larger stars.
1 billion years			Red dwarf now fully formed. Average surface temperature might reach only about 4,900°F (2,700°C) – cool for a star.

15 times as much mass as our Sun, a star of about the size and mass as our Sun, and a star with about a third of our Sun's mass. After only several million years have passed, the life of the 15-solar-mass giant star is nearly over, as it explodes in a supernova. Meanwhile, the other two stars have barely begun their lives.

Time from Nebula Stage	Average Star (1 solar mass)	Small Star (1/3 solar mass)
4.6 billion years	The star is now just like our Sun. As star uses up its hydrogen, its temperature and size slowly increase.	
12 billion years	Star begins to consume its helium, and balloons into a red giant. By now, any planets once suitable for life – like Earth – have long ago been turned into lifeless wastelands. At its largest, this star may extend as far out as the orbit of Earth!	The giant star has been "dead" for well over 10 billion years. The star like our Sun is starting to expand into a red giant. But the red dwarf – slow, steady, and stable – is still just starting its life.
12.4 billion years	As star uses up its fuel, it shrinks into a white dwarf only about as big as Earth.	
50-100 billion years	As far as we know, the Universe is only 13.7 billion years old. But we think that the white dwarf may burn out completely in many billions of years – and become a black dwarf.	Red dwarf stars might burn on quietly for perhaps as long as 100 billion years. They might become tiny white dwarfs. No one knows for certain.

More Books about Stars

The Birth of Our Universe. Isaac Asimov (Gareth Stevens)

The Life and Death of Stars. Ray Spangenburg and Kit Moser (Franklin Watts)

Star Factories: The Birth of Stars and Planets. Ray Jayawardhana (Raintree Steck-Vaughn)

Stars and Planets Atlas. Ian Ridpath (Facts on File)

The Sun. Isaac Asimov (Gareth Stevens)

Superstar: The Supernova of 1987. Franklyn M. Branle and True Kelley (Harpercollins)

DVDs

Atlas of the Sky. (Space Holdings)

Stargaze II - Visions of the Universe. (Wea)

Web Sites

The Internet is a good place to get more information about the stars. The web sites listed here can help you learn about the most recent discoveries, as well as those made in the past.

NASA, Imagine the Universe. imagine.gsfc.nasa.gov/docs/science/science.html

Nine Planets. www.nineplanets.org/sol.html

Solar Views. www.nineplanets.org/sol.html

University of Wisconsin, The Constellations and Their Stars.
www.astro.wisc.edu/~dolan/constellations/

Windows to the Universe. www.windows.ucar.edu/tour/link=/the_universe/the_universe.html

Places to Visit

Here are some museums and centers where you can find a variety of exhibits and shows about the stars.

Adler Planetarium and Astronomy Museum
1300 S. Lake Shore Drive
Chicago, IL 60605-2403

American Museum of Natural History
Rose Center for Earth and Space
Central Park West at 79th Street
New York, NY 10024

Carter Observatory
40 Salamanca Rd
Kelburn
Wellington
New Zealand

Museum of Science, Boston
Science Park
Boston, MA 02114

National Air and Space Museum
Smithsonian Institution
6th and Independence Avenue SW
Washington, DC 20560

Scienceworks Museum
2 Booker Street
Spotswood
Melbourne, Victoria 3015
Australia

Glossary

astronomer: a person involved in the scientific study of the Universe and its various celestial bodies.

Big Bang: a huge explosion that scientists believe created our Universe about 13.7 billion years ago.

black dwarf star: a "dead" star. When a star like our Sun uses up its store of hydrogen fuel and collapses, it becomes a white dwarf star. When a white dwarf cools off completely, it becomes a black dwarf.

black hole: a tightly packed object with such powerful gravity that not even light can escape from it.

constellation: a grouping of stars in the sky that seems to trace out a familiar pattern, figure, or symbol.

galaxy: a large star system containing up to hundreds of billions of stars, along with gas and dust. Our Galaxy is known as the Milky Way.

helium: a light, colorless gas that makes up part of every star.

hydrogen: a colorless, odorless gas that is the simplest and lightest of the elements. Most stars are originally largely hydrogen.

light-year: the distance that light travels in one year — nearly 6 trillion miles (9.5 trillion km).

luminous: giving off light or other electromagnetic radiation.

main sequence: a class of stars that shows a stable relationship between brightness, size, and temperature; the stage of a star's life which our Sun is at.

nebula: a cloud of dust and gas in space. Some nebulas, or nebulae, are the birthplaces of stars, and some are the debris of dying stars.

neutrino: an extremely tiny particle produced in certain nuclear reactions, such as when hydrogen fuses to form helium in the center of a star.

neutron star: a star that has as much mass as an ordinary star, but the mass — consisting mainly of the nuclear particles called neutrons — is squeezed into a small ball.

nuclear fusion: the smashing together of highly heated atoms to create larger atoms, such as the fusion of hydrogen atoms to produce helium atoms. The process releases huge amounts of energy.

planetary nebula: a shell of gas expelled by a red giant star that has used up much of its hydrogen fuel, leaving the star's core as a white dwarf.

proto-: the earliest or first form of something. In this book, a young star is a "protostar."

radiation: the spreading of heat, light, or other forms of energy by rays or waves.

red dwarf star: a cool, faint star, smaller than our Sun. Red dwarfs are probably the most numerous stars in our Galaxy, but they are so faint that they are extremely difficult to see.

red giant: a large bright star that represents a late stage in the life of a star like our Sun, when its hydrogen fuel has run low and the star has expanded, with its outer layers becoming a cooler red.

supernova: the explosive collapse of a very large star, which ends up as a neutron star or black hole.

white dwarf star: the small star that remains when a star uses up its store of nuclear fuel and collapses but does not explode.

Index

Born in 1920, Isaac Asimov came to the United States as a young boy from his native Russia. As a young man, he was a student of biochemistry. In time, he became one of the most productive writers the world has ever known. His books cover a spectrum of topics, including science, history, language theory, fantasy, and science fiction. His brilliant imagination gained him the respect and admiration of adults and children alike. Sadly, Isaac Asimov died shortly after the publication of the first edition of *Isaac Asimov's Library of the Universe.*

The publishers wish to thank the following for permission to reproduce copyright material: front cover, 3, © Mark Paternostro 1988; 4, 5, © Paul Dimare 1988; 6, Jet Propulsion Laboratory; 7, 11 (both), 18 (both), 24 (both), National Optical Astronomy Observatories; 8, 17 (inset), Courtesy of NRAO/AUI; 9, Lick Observatory; 10, © Mathew Groshek 1980; 12, © Brian Sullivan 1989; 13 (upper), © Allan Morton; 13 (lower), Sharon Burris/© Gareth Stevens, Inc.; 14 (large), © Paul Dimare; 14 (inset), NASA Marshall Space Flight Center; 15, Andrea Dupree (Harvard-Smithsonian CfA), Ronald Gilliland (STScI), NASA, and ESA; 16, NASA/HST/J. Morse/K. Davidson; 17 (large), © 1993 by Richard Wainscoat and John Kormendy, Institute for Astronomy, University of Hawaii; 19, Dr. Christopher Burrows, ESA/STScI and NASA; 20, © Lynette Cook 1988; 21, NASA/CXC/HST/ASU/J. Hester et al.; 22 (all), 23, 25 (upper), © John Foster; 25 (lower), © 1984/University of Hawaii Institute of Astronomy, by Jack Marling and Wayne Annala, 24"f/15 telescope; 26, NASA; 27, © Greg Mort 1987.